Mommy is Sick
What do you do?

Marcia Ashford

copyright 2019 Heartstring Productions, LLC
All rights reserved. No part of this publication may be reproduced or used in any manner without written permission of the author
with the exception for using brief quotations embodied
in articles and reviews.

Dedicated to our Daddy Bear
Randy Ashford

what do you do?

Read her a story

Make hot chocolate

say 'I love you'

Let her sleep. Better yet...

All those things Mommy does for you when you are sick?

She loves them too.
Giggle giggle.

Daddy is sick. What do you do?

www.ingramcontent.com/pod-product-compliance
Lightning Source LLC
Chambersburg PA
CBHW041155290426
44108CB00002B/83